LET'S GET A PET!

MY FIRST FISH

By Joan Stoltman

Gareth Stevens
PUBLISHING

Please visit our website, www.garethstevens.com. For a free color catalog of all our high-quality books, call toll free 1-800-542-2595 or fax 1-877-542-2596.

Cataloging-in-Publication Data

Names: Stoltman, Joan.
Title: My first fish / Joan Stoltman.
Description: New York : Gareth Stevens Publishing, 2018. | Series: Let's get a pet! | Includes index.
Identifiers: ISBN 9781482464535 (pbk.) | ISBN 9781482464559 (library bound) | ISBN 9781482464542 (6 pack)
Subjects: LCSH: Aquarium fishes–Juvenile literature. | Pets–Juvenile literature.
Classification: LCC SF457.25 S76 2018 | DDC 639.34–dc23

Published in 2018 by
Gareth Stevens Publishing
111 East 14th Street, Suite 349
New York, NY 10003

Designer: Bethany Perl
Editor: Joan Stoltman

Photo credits: Cover, p. 1 Elena Blokhina/Shutterstock.com; pp. 2–24 (background texture) Liliya Mulyukova/Shutterstock.com; p. 5 Sukpaiboonwat/Shutterstock.com; p. 7 underworld/Shutterstock.com; p. 9 (goldfish, guppy) SOMMAI/Shutterstock.com; p. 9 (betta) Boonchuay1970/Shutterstock.com; p. 9 (pleco) Mirko Rosenau/Shutterstock.com; p. 11 LAKRUWAN WANNIARACHCHI/AFP/Getty Images; p. 13 Andrey Armyagov/Shutterstock.com; p. 15 S-F/Shutterstock.com; p. 17 (main image) Trueblackheart/Shutterstock.com; pp. 17 (inset), 19 Mirko Rosenau/Shutterstock.com; p. 21 wavebreakmedia/Shutterstock.com.

Printed in China

CPSIA compliance information: Batch #CS17GS: For further information contact Gareth Stevens, New York, New York at 1-800-542-2595.

CONTENTS

Boldface words appear in the glossary.

Why Get a Fish?

A fish is a great pet! There are hundreds of kinds of fish in all sorts of sizes, colors, and shapes. Every day with a pet fish is a chance to learn something new as you watch it **explore** its world!

Fish Are Amazing!

Fish are really smart! They can recognize each other. They even talk to each other! Fish use buzzes, clicks, and other sounds to talk and tell each other how they're feeling. People can only hear them if they use special science tools.

Freshwater or Salt Water?

Fish can live in either **freshwater** or salt water. Saltwater **tanks** are hard to keep up and take a lot of time. If this is your family's first pet fish, it may be best to start with freshwater fish.

FRESHWATER FISH

BETTA

PLECO

GUPPY

GOLDFISH

Where to Put the Tank

Since you'll want to watch your new pet fish a lot, put your new tank in the room where your family spends the most time. Wherever the tank ends up, know that bright lights and loud noises can scare fish.

Time to Decorate!

One of the greatest things about having a pet fish is **decorating** the new tank! Your pet fish will be happiest in a tank that looks like its natural **habitat**. Use rocks, wood, and glass objects to create spaces for your pet fish to hide and explore!

You can even have some kinds of living plants in your tank! They help keep the water healthy for the fish and are a great place for your pet fish to hide. And they'll look lovely!

JAVA FERN

Time to Eat!

Fish need to eat, of course! There are many different types of fish food, including **flakes** and frozen food. Some fish like flies and worms! Others like to snack on vegetables such as a cucumber or potato!

FISH FOOD
TABLETS
FISH
FLAKES
BLOODWORMS

How to Feed a Fish

Many fish need to eat two or three times a day. Helping with feedings is a great way to help out with your new pet! Be careful to only feed your fish as much as it can eat in 1 minute.

FISH FLAKES

Keeping Your Fish Safe

You can pet many other kinds of animals, but you can't pet fish. It hurts them! Also, fish get very scared when you knock on their tank. You can help keep your fish safe and happy by checking the tank for **cracks** and **leaks**, too!

GLOSSARY

crack: a break

decorate: to make something look nice by adding extra objects to it

explore: to search in order to find new things

flake: a small, flat, thin piece of food

freshwater: water that isn't salty

habitat: the natural place where an animal or plant lives

leak: a break that lets the water out

tank: a glass or plastic box filled with water

FOR MORE INFORMATION

BOOKS

Amstutz, Lisa J. *Fish*. North Mankato, MN: Capstone Press, 2017.

Bergin, Mark. *It's Fun to Draw Sea Creatures*. New York, NY: Skyhorse Publishing, 2013.

Carr, Aaron. *Fish*. New York, NY: AV2 by Weigl, 2012.

WEBSITES

Aquascapes
petdoggames.com/game/a/aquascapes/aquascapes.html
Create your dream aquarium online!

Can Fish Breathe Underwater?
discoverykids.com/articles/can-fish-breathe-underwater/
Read this article about fish!

Fun Fish Facts for Kids
sciencekids.co.nz/sciencefacts/animals/fish.html
Learn all about fish!

Publisher's note to educators and parents: Our editors have carefully reviewed these websites to ensure that they are suitable for students. Many websites change frequently, however, and we cannot guarantee that a site's future contents will continue to meet our high standards of quality and educational value. Be advised that students should be closely supervised whenever they access the Internet.

INDEX